À ma femme, Amy, et à mes deux garçons, pour le bonheur que vous me procurez chaque jour. Je vous aime et vous souhaite du bonheur, pour toujours et à jamais. - Michael

Suivez-nous pour tout savoir sur les nouveaux livres et les concours sur PiccoPuppy.com et @PiccoPuppy sur Facebook et Instagram.
#iwishyouhappinessbook #piccopuppy

Un merci tout particulier à Ann Baratashvili, pour ses magnifiques illustrations ; à David Miles, pour sa magnifique conception de la couverture et ses précieux conseils ; à George Willms, pour la merveilleuse traduction française ; et à Émilie Cossette, Marie Reilhac, Maël Paradis et Eve Garant pour la correction des épreuves.

Crédits pour les polices de caractères
Lost Brush par Stripes Studio
Marck Script de Denis Masharov
Cormorant Upright de Christian Thalmann
Century Schoolbook de Morris Fuller Benton
Copse de Dan Rhatigan
Josefin Sans de Santiago Orozco

Première publication en 2021 par Picco Puppy
Marketing Munch Pty Ltd DBA Picco Puppy, PO Box 103 Killara NSW 2071 Australie
Picco Puppy est une marque déposée de Marketing Munch Pty Ltd

ISBN 978-1-925973-96-9

Dedicated to my wife, Amy, and two boys, for the happiness you give me every day. I love you and wish you happiness, forever and ever. –Michael

Follow us for news of new books and giveaways at PiccoPuppy.com and @PiccoPuppy on Facebook and Instagram.
#iwishyouhappinessbook #piccopuppy

Special thanks to Ann Baratashvili, for your beautiful illustrations; David Miles, for your beautiful cover design and invaluable guidance; George Willms, for the wonderful French translation; and Émilie Cossette, Marie Reilhac, Maël Paradis, and Eve Garant for the proofreading.

Font Credits
Lost Brush by Stripes Studio
Marck Script by Denis Masharov
Cormorant Upright by Christian Thalmann
Century Schoolbook by Morris Fuller Benton
Copse by Dan Rhatigan
Josefin Sans by Santiago Orozco

First published in 2021 by Picco Puppy
Marketing Munch Pty Ltd DBA Picco Puppy, PO Box 103 Killara NSW 2071 Australia
Picco Puppy® is a registered trademark of Marketing Munch Pty Ltd

Je te souhaite du bonheur

I Wish You Happiness

MICHAEL WONG • ANN BARATASHVILI

Je te souhaite des *rêves*
et des *aspirations*, de
déployer tes ailes et de
viser les étoiles.

I wish you *dreams* and
aspirations, to spread
your wings and reach
for the stars.

Je te souhaite du *courage*
et de la *force*, car la magie
commence au-delà de ta
zone de confort.

I wish you *courage* and
strength, for the magic
begins at the end of your
comfort zone.

Je te souhaite *imagination*
et *créativité*, car le monde est
une toile blanche où tu peux
peindre ton chef-d'œuvre.

I wish you *imagination*
and *creativity*, for the
world is a blank canvas to
paint your masterpiece.

Je te souhaite de l'*aventure*
et de la *curiosité*, pour aller
là où il n'y a pas de chemin
et y tracer un sentier.

I wish you *adventure*
and *curiosity*, to go
where there is no path
and leave a trail.

Je te souhaite *santé* et *bien-être*, car ils valent plus que toutes les richesses du monde.

I wish you *health* and *well-being*, for they are worth more than all the riches in the world.

Je te souhaite *paix* et *tranquillité*, d'écouter
les oiseaux et de contempler les étoiles.

I wish you *peace* and *tranquility*, to
listen to the birds and gaze at the stars.

Je te souhaite
connaissance et *sagesse*,
car ce sont les bases
d'une vie réussie.

I wish you *knowledge*
and *wisdom*, for they
are the foundations of a
successful life.

Je te souhaite de la
persévérance et de la *résilience*,
de ne jamais abandonner.

I wish you *grit* and
resilience, to never
ever give up.

Je te souhaite *succès*
et *prospérité*, d'avoir
confiance en toi et en ta
capacité à réussir.

I wish you *success*
and *prosperity*, to
trust yourself and your
ability to succeed.

Je te souhaite de la *chance*
et des *opportunités*,
car plus tu essaieras, plus
chanceux tu seras.

I wish you *luck* and
opportunity, for
the more you try, the
luckier you get.

Je te souhaite *foi* et *espoir*, afin
de croire que tout ira bien.

I wish you *faith* and *hope*, to
believe everything will be all right.

Je te souhaite *famille* et *amitié*, car ce sont les plus grandes sources de bonheur de la vie.

I wish you *family* and *friendships*, for they are life's greatest sources of happiness.

Je te souhaite de la joie et du rire, de rire longtemps et fort jusqu'à en perdre le souffle.

I wish you *joy* and *laughter*,
to laugh long and loud until
you gasp for breath.

Je te souhaite de la *gentillesse*
et de la *générosité*, car aucun
acte de bonté n'est jamais perdu,
aussi petit soit-il.

I wish you *kindness* and
generosity, for no act of
kindness is ever wasted, no
matter how small.

Je te souhaite de l'*amour*
et de l'*affection*, pour
remplir ton bon cœur d'un
océan de joie.

I wish you *love* and
affection, to fill your
beautiful heart with an
ocean of joy.

Je te souhaite toutes ces merveilleuses choses, mais surtout . . .

Je te souhaite *du bonheur !*

I wish you all those wonderful things, but most of all . . .

I wish you *happiness!*

Peux-tu trouver ces personnes célèbres ?

Quels que soient les obstacles que tu rencontres, crois en toi et en qui tu es, comme l'ont fait ces personnes célèbres. Peux-tu trouver les cinq personnes présentes dans ce livre ?

Peux-tu trouver un jeune Neil Armstrong ?
Neil est un célèbre astronaute qui est devenu la première personne à marcher sur la lune en 1969. Avant cela, il était pilote d'essai de recherche expérimentale, ce qui est un métier très dangereux.

Peux-tu trouver une jeune Katherine Johnson ?
Katherine est une mathématicienne dont les calculs ont contribué à envoyer la fusée Apollo 11 transportant Neil Armstrong et ses collègues astronautes sur la lune.

Peux-tu trouver une jeune Amelia Earhart ?
Amelia a été la première aviatrice à traverser l'océan Atlantique en solo. Elle a contribué à la création de The Ninety-Nines, une organisation internationale de femmes pilotes.

Peux-tu trouver une jeune J. K. Rowling ?
Douze éditeurs ont rejeté le premier livre de Joanne. Elle a dû attendre un an avant que son livre ne soit finalement publié. Ses livres Harry Potter sont devenus la série de livres la plus vendue de l'histoire.

Peux-tu trouver un jeune Alexander Selkirk ?
Alexander est célèbre pour avoir passé quatre ans comme naufragé sur une île inhabitée. Son histoire de survie a inspiré le roman Robinson Crusoé de Daniel Defoe, souvent considéré comme le premier roman anglais, publié en 1719.

Can You Spot the Famous People?

No matter what obstacles you face, believe in yourself and all that you are—just like these famous people did. Can you spot all five in the book?

Can you spot a young Neil Armstrong?
Neil is a famous astronaut who became the first person to walk on the moon in 1969. Before that, he was an experimental research test pilot, which is a very dangerous job.

Can you spot a young Katherine Johnson?
Katherine is a mathematician whose calculations helped send the Apollo 11 rocket carrying Neil Armstrong and his fellow astronauts to the moon.

Can you spot a young Amelia Earhart?
Amelia was the first female aviator to fly solo across the Atlantic Ocean. She helped to create The Ninety-Nines, an international organization of women pilots.

Can you spot a young J. K. Rowling?
Twelve publishers rejected Joanne's first book. She had to wait a year before her book was finally published. Her Harry Potter books went on to become the best-selling book series in history.

Can you spot a young Alexander Selkirk?
Alexander famously spent four years as a castaway on an uninhabited island. His survival story inspired Daniel Defoe's Robinson Crusoe, often credited as the first English novel, published in 1719.

Peux-tu trouver ces chiens ?

Il y a dix-sept chiens et un chat dans le livre. Peux-tu les retrouver tous ?

Beagle

Épagneul Cavalier King Charles

Dalmatien

Bouledogue français

Berger allemand

Golden retriever

Terrier Jack Russell

Labrador retriever

Maltais

Poméranien

Caniche

Carlin

Saint-bernard

Shiba Inu

Chat Siamois

Corgi gallois

Terrier du West Highland

Terrier du Yorkshire

Can You Spot the Dogs?

There are seventeen dogs and one cat in the book. Can you spot them all?

Beagle

Cavalier King Charles Spaniel

Dalmatian

French Bulldog

German Shepherd

Golden Retriever

Jack Russell Terrier

Labrador Retriever

Maltese

Pomeranian

Poodle

Pug

Saint Bernard

Shiba Inu

Siamese Cat

Welsh Corgi

West Highland Terrier

Yorkshire Terrier

More Michael Wong Books

A curious young boy spends the summer with his grandma, asking big questions about life. Drawing on her wisdom, experiences, and even a few regrets, Grandma answers with love and honesty.
This heartwarming book invites grandparents and parents to share their own stories and hard-earned life lessons — too precious to be forgotten.
The beautifully crafted hardcover edition is available on Amazon.

Picco Puppy hardcovers are available in personalized and bilingual editions in Spanish, French, Italian, and German at PiccoPuppy.com.

Win a hardcover every month! Claim your gift at www.PiccoPuppy.com/gift

Michael Wong is an award-winning children's author. He is passionate about creating beautiful, empowering, diverse, and inclusive books for children. Michael lives with his wife and two children in Sydney, Australia.

Ann Baratashvili is an illustrator and concept artist. She won first prize in the 2009 DeviantArt/Wacom "Bring Your Vision to Life: Dreams" contest. Ann lives with her husband and son in Tbilisi, Georgia.

The Unconditional Love Series

La série amour inconditionnel

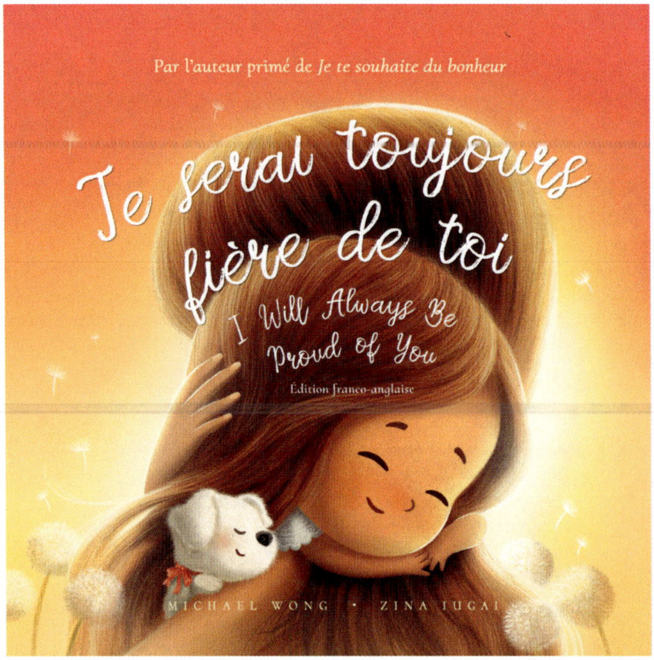

Made in the USA
Las Vegas, NV
22 June 2026

49344101R00026